IF YOUR NET WORTH IS LOWER NOW THAN
IT WAS LAST YEAR HERE'S THE WAY TO
MAKE MONEY IN TODAY'S MARKET

Get Back Up!

LESSONS FROM SURFING
TO REBUILD YOUR CRASHING PORTFOLIO

A Thinking Press
Book by
Bill Shepard

Get Back Up!
Lessons from surfing to rebuild your crashing portfolio.

Bill Shepard

Thinking Press Books
an Imprint of Mindgarden Group Publishing
606 Commercial Ave, Suite C
Anacortes, WA 98221

ISBN 13: 9781439225530
ISBN10: 1-4392-2553-2

This book is version 1.0.1
Updated Editions will be available from www.fromsurfing.com. Your password to access the members updates site is inside the body of the book. Check the password instructions on the website.

Printed and Bound in the United States of America.

About this WEB (Web Enabled Book)

This is a small book by design. But it's also the portal to a larger learning community.

Whether you are a sophisticated trader or just getting started, you'll find that the twenty two insights in this book will guide you to being a better investor every day. Building up your mental game as it were.

But even the most profound right brain ideas are only useful when they can be put into action by left brain practical application. My experience is that learning to apply new learning is best engaged with other students of the craft. So we offer that at the companion website to this book www.fromsurfing.com.

Your password to access the book owner exclusive content is inside. But more on that later.

Let's get started.

Contents

Preface

That Was Just A Dream Some Of Us Had
JONI MITCHELL – CALIFORNIA FROM THE CD BLUE

In the Fall of 2007 world equity markets peaked and then rolled over. For the first time in our lifetime we entered a long term Bear Market[1] and all the old rules for investing went out the window.

Unfortunately, like the dinosaurs after the comet hit, a lot of people haven't realized how different it is this time and haven't changed their investment approach. If that's you and you're watching, paralyzed in agony, as your investment accounts continue to get demolished, don't despair.

What this book provides is a new set of financial metaphors to manage your investing and get you out of your current mess. A new way of thinking as it were. Surprisingly, those metaphors come from surfing.

How did I stumble upon them?

Recently I was talking with a trading friend who was struggling in positions[2] that she felt were good but "early" (that's trader talk* for mistaken).

She felt she needed to be trading. But the market direction was working against her strategy and she was losing money.

Still, she kept trying to force it to work and kept getting more and more frustrated as her losses were continuing to grow.

As we talked I found myself telling her, "the market is like the ocean, it will be there tomorrow" and that's when it clicked.

---

* I've chosen to not explain financial terms or concepts in the main text of the book so as not to interrupt the flow. But wherever it seems appropriate I've placed an end note reference at the first use of what may be an unfamiliar term or concept so you can skip to the back and get a quick definition as well as references for more information.

Get Back Up!

It's nature's way of telling you.
Something's wrong.

LYRICS BY RANDY CALIFORNIA

Denial.

No, it's not a river in Egypt. It's what holds us back when it's time to move on.

Before we can see a new way of thinking there is usually an old way of thinking that has to be un-learned.

Like many people, it took me a while to realize that the old verities of, "Hold on in rough times, because the market will come back even stronger" just aren't true anymore[3]. But even after I "realized" that was no longer true, I habitually and unconsciously reverted back to patterns of bull market thinking.

And those old patterns of thinking kept tripping me up, causing me to make poor investment decisions.

In other words, the bull market was in my unconscious and I needed a way to rewrite my brain's patterned responses.

What I came to realize was that I was no longer on a tide of rising equities that would over time inexorably move everything forward. Not anymore.

Today we're in a long term Bear Market and that requires a different way of thinking and a different way of managing our investments.

The market isn't against us individually per se. It just needs to unwind a lot of excesses that have built up over a number of decades.[4]

So while the market is correcting itself there are plenty of strategies where we can make money. What we need is a changed way of thinking to be able to take advantage of them.

But the first step is to get really honest with yourself. Instead of denying the condition your investments are in today, admit it. To yourself. To your significant other. To anyone that will hold you accountable for fixing it.

Then decide that you're willing to do whatever it takes to succeed in this changed environment and rebuild your crashed portfolio.

Which brings us to surfboards.

If you are currently managing all your investment accounts yourself you don't need this chapter. The rest of the book is for you.
But if you still have others directing your investments you need to ask yourself . . .

What color is your surfboard?

Surfing is honest.

When you surf it's just you and your board on the ocean.

You can try a longboard to help you catch more waves. Or you can go to a short board to catch the drop on steeper waves. But there's no coach standing behind you giving you tips. No autopilot of balance to keep you from falling.

When you are a retail investor[5] it's that way too. It's just you and your account out in the wide open marketplace.

There's lot's of tools available but that scary feeling of being out on our own has caused many of us to try and find someone we could hire to guide our investing to guaranteed profitability. In most cases, we've outsourced our investments, particularly our retirement accounts to "experts" because we've been told that investing was way too complicated for the ordinary person. And to be honest we gladly abdicated that responsibility.

For most of the last several decades those retirement accounts grew on the natural rising tide of a bull market carrying your account up with it. In most cases your advisor could make money by just not making stupid mistakes.

But now in a market that is carrying everything down and with huge losses in your portfolio what are you going to do?

You have two choices to make at this point. First, you can hope that the experts who have not been able to prevent you from getting into this mess can now get you out of it.

Or you can choose to take charge of your investment and retirement accounts and get out of this mess yourself.

But wait you say, I have a full time job and family obligations and church and social obligations. I don't have time to learn how to manage my investments.

Poor you. It may not be what we'd like but it's where we are. So buck up and let's get on with it.

The good news is that learning to manage your investments isn't that hard. Yes it takes time and focused attention. But so does learning to do anything well. You don't have to learn everything before you can start. With just a few basic but significant changes you can get to the place where you are not losing any more and that in itself is probably better than what's going on now.

The second choice you have to make is to choose to be a trader in a trader's market and an investor in an investor's market. If you keep trying to buy and hold in this bear market you will find yourself going down.

You will have to learn how to trade.

By that I mean you will have to actively make choices to buy and sell and stay on top of them. And keep doing that again and again. But just that act of deciding to learn how to actively manage your investments will be a positive change. And I'm pretty sure it won't take long for you to find out how energizing trading is.

The good news is that there are a thousand great ways to trade and make money. Stocks. Options. Futures, Currencies. Commodities[6]. The list goes on and on with something to suit every temperament and every trading capability.

But the first and most important decision you need to make is that you are ready and committed to take charge of your financial future and decide . . .
 . . . what color is your surfboard?

Get Back Up!

The Ocean will be there tomorrow.

Why do we stay in losing investments?

Psychologists have lots of reasons to explain that, but I think one of the reasons is because we have been emotionally conditioned by "investment advisors" of all types to believe that we always have to be in the market. To have our money working for us.

Why?

It's easy to see why that may be in "their" best interest. They make commissions when we are in their vehicles but don't when we aren't.

But our question should be, what's in our best interest?

I didn't realize the power of that question until I was at an investor group conference and had a market maker[7] from the CBOE[8] pits tell me, "You know you retail traders really have an advantage over us. You don't have to be in the market all the time like we do."

I had never thought of that before. But it was true. If the market conditions and our methods of trading aren't in an advantageous position we as retail investors can just step aside and wait until conditions are in our favor.

This guy, who I thought was a Master of The Universe, had to play every day. In every market condition. So what if it's a Category 5 hurricane? He has to be buying and selling. Same goes for hedge fund managers, the proverbial brightest bulbs in the chandelier. And mutual fund managers, they have it even worse because they not only have to stay in but they have to follow their funds defined strategy. Can you say "I've fallen in the emerging market meltdown and I can't get up?" Ouch!

Here's another thought experiment. If I'm in cash[9] and the market drops 30% carrying every stock down with it at more or less the same rate, how much more stock can I buy after that drop? Yep, a lot more.

Even worse, if my portfolio is decimated by 40% like most 401K's were in 2008 how much do I have to grow to get back to even? The painful answer is 80%.

That's the power of being in cash in a declining market no matter if you are day trading or deciding how to invest your 401K.

What matters more to you, what your financial adviser thinks about you or how much money is in your account? Would you rather have cocktail hour stories or an undamaged portfolio?

If in January 2008 you had told your 401K adviser

to go to cash after your portfolio had dropped by 10% he would have told you that you were going to miss the rebound. And that was a real possibility.

The problem was that no matter how much happy talk was out there, the market was going down. The charts were all moving from the upper left to the lower right. All of them.

So staying invested made money for your advisors but you lost money. But if you had moved to cash you would have been able to buy a third more shares of now lower priced stock by the end of that year when the market started turning back up into growth mode again.

So what can I tell myself when I'm afraid of missing a possible future opportunity?

Like the ocean, the market will be there tomorrow.

What that means is I can let the trade I'm not confident in and not prepared for, pass me by. I can remain calm because I know I can have just as much fun and be just as profitable tomorrow when I'll be clear headed and not emotionally on edge. And I can be as prepared as I should have been today.

And more importantly, if I'm in a trade or an investment that is working against me and I'm getting all bollixed up I can make it not get any worse. I can close that trade for whatever loss I have to take and go to cash. Then I can take a time out and get my bearings to figure out what a good trade opportunity will be and start making money with that.

The Ocean will be there tomorrow.

Ride the waves the ocean gives you.

Second Big Lesson.

You've heard the old expression

*To a man with a hammer
everything looks like a nail.*

It was often that way for me with trading.

When I learn something new that works for me, ba-da-bing I just want to keep doing it. The problem comes when the market changes and I don't notice.

I'm in a group of pretty sophisticated traders who are masters at Iron Condors. If you're not an options trader, don't worry about it. An Iron Condor is a trade that uses four different options at the same time to make money from differences in time decay. It sounds complicated but it's not. It's a great trade for generating monthly income with a high probability of success.

The other nice thing about Iron Condors is that they make money when a market goes up or when a market goes down. Up to a point. When you get beyond that point Condors get really ugly, really quick.

What happened was that most of these pretty sophisticated traders learned to do their Iron Condors in relatively low volatility[10] markets. Ten out twelve months of the year they could make ten to fifteen percent per month. As long as they held their losses to no more than ten percent in the two losing months it was a great system.

But as this bear market roared in and took markets over the waterfall without the benefit of a barrel, a lot of these guys got hurt. I say these guys but I was in there with them.

Once again, a previous history of success had patterned a set of expectations that didn't serve us well in a new environment.

Which led me to my next insight,

Ride the waves the ocean gives you

I know. Duh!!

But really. Ask yourself honestly, how well do you do at assessing the market every day without preconceptions?

When you look at the price chart of a stock you own and has been losing money, do you look at it affectionately and see opportunity when it isn't really there? You wouldn't be the first to say, "I know the arrows are all pointing down now but I believe it's about to turn up."

On the other hand, does your desire for a falling market that you can short[25] lead you to see one coming even when it's not there? Or does your desire to return to the good old days of a bull market make you jump in to "buy at the bottom" when the market is still just clearly going down?

There's a quote that is attributed to John Maynard Keynes

The market can stay irrational longer than you can stay solvent.

It rings true for us because we have all been there, trying to tell ourselves we were right the whole time the market was telling us we were wrong.

I'm not saying give up on stock charts or market signals[11]. As traders we need those to navigate our way like the stars that guided the ancient mariners. In fact in these whacky markets we need them even more.

What I am saying though is don't let anything blind you to what's really going on in the market and be ready to . . .

. . . ride the waves the ocean gives you.

Size matters and smaller is better.

Small.

In our culture that's not usually something to brag about. Start telling acquaintances, "I'm small these days." And you'll get those "I'm so sorry for you" looks.

But just a while back I heard a trader who writes one of the top internationally respected newsletters tell his audience,

I'm a greybeard in this industry. I've been trading for over 35 years and I've never seen a market like this. It's time to get small. Very very small. [12]

What he was saying wasn't just a batten down the hatches and escape to cash strategy. (Even though you know that's a smart move sometimes).

No, what he was saying is that in periods of high volatility the best risk management strategists realize that their leverage is much higher and correspondingly their risk/reward opportunity is higher as well.

What that means is, while you can lose a lot, you can also make the same amount of money each month as you used to, but with far fewer dollars in the game.

So how to trade that? That is the question that matters, right?

Easy. Start trading smaller size trades and shorter time frames in a proportion that generates you the same dollar opportunity as you used to get when you traded larger just a few years ago.

I know. Another Duh! but really easy to miss.

If you trade currencies you know they are moving at rates of change in weeks that used to take months or even years. So cut your size proportionally. Trading one tenth what you used to per trade isn't too small.

I know, it's going to be impossible not to keep hearing that voice in the back of your mind telling you how much more you could have made if you'd traded at your old size when the trade is going with you. But when it goes against you your losses won't eat up overnight what you made over the last three months.

That's the time to speak back to that voice and tell it, "See! I told you so . . .
. . . size matters and smaller is better."

Fall small.

There's a corollary to the size issue and that's how well you manage your trades that go wrong.

In surfing when you know you are going to fall you can ditch the ride and dive into the wave. Except when you are in a competition bailing out has little consequence and lets you keep riding the rest of the day. On the other hand, the more you try and contort yourself to get back in balance and save the ride usually makes things worse. You end up "over the falls" in the front of the board where the crashing wave spends a while pummeling you like an unbalanced load in the spin cycle of your washer.

Anybody who has surfed has been there and done that and frankly doesn't look forward to repeating the experience.

Same with trading. When you know a trade has gone bad what do you do? Do you grit your teeth and tell yourself you can ride it out, the market is bound to turn your direction eventually? Or do you start flailing to try and whip your trade around and make it work? Or, do you have a predefined strategy for bailing on failed trades so you don't get hurt?

I'll know I've achieved mastery as a trader when I can coolly and calmly fall small and ride long. I'm getting better at that.

Most traders I know who are successful tell me that the key to being able to keep their losses small is to have a written plan for every day that includes the specifics for how they will decide the trade is going wrong and what to do. And then they follow that plan without letting their emotions override them.

For swing traders[13] that daily plan may be a modified carry over from a plan that was made several days ago and slightly updated each day. But the plan for when to bail out is updated every day as the days go by.

Every trader has a different hit rate for successes but every trader knows that a reasonable percentage of all the trades they make are going to fail.

The key to overall success is to have a plan for more successes than failures and to learn how to . . .
. . . fall small.

Get Back Up!

You can always try another beach.

One of the most liberating changes I made this year was the SPY. The SPY is not some secret agent thing. It's the Exchange Traded Fund (ETF) for the S&P 500.

Yep it was that simple.

I was trying to trade option spreads[14] on individual stocks and they were killing me. It wasn't my fault. I was doing my homework. And it wasn't their fault because the battering they were getting wasn't because of what they were doing.

The market had changed from being fundamentals[15] and technicals[16] driven to being purely news driven. And retail traders like you and me are always the last ones to get in on the news.

A fellow trader suggested that I try switching from individual stocks to trading the market as a whole because of their built in diversity and relatively calmer moves.

The SPY was the perfect candidate. It's an ETF that

is traded in penny wide spreads[17] and is likely the most liquid equity on the globe.

I switched to trading SPY and "ahhhhh" what a difference.

What I realized is that suggestion from my friend was like getting a call on my cell phone from a buddy saying, "You gotta get down here. They're killing on Hialeah Bay."

So the simple lesson you should always ask yourself is, "How's it feeling?" If your pulse is racing and your hands are sweating you're probably not on the right beach for you. Find a place where you have a good sense that you know where things are going.

For most people that's the broad markets, the Dow and the S&P. Then when things feel more under control and you're looking for more aggressive trades look at market sector[18] ETF's. If the financials are moving into rotation you can ride that faster wave for a little extra juice. Feeling even smarter? Then trade some individual stocks.

But when it starts feeling scary again, see if there is something at a level up that is averaging out the individual or sector choppiness.

And remember . . .
. . . you can always try another beach.

Get Back Up!

You can't catch a wave you've missed,
so stop paddling.

Chasing.

Easy to say. Tough not to do.

I think the reason why it's hard not to chase a trade that's passed us by is that we often can't see its real trajectory. We get tempted to chase at the point where we realize, "Hey, that's a great trade." But by then it's already too late to get in.

It helps me to remember what it was like when I was first learning to surf. Sitting on the board. The pattern of the swells coming in and that timing and motion judgment that says "This will be good one, let's go."

Then I'd paddle like mad and realize as the wave slid away beneath me that I'd missed it.

Over time and with practice every surfer learns to "feel" when to launch out and just how hard to paddle to catch the momentum. Pretty soon it looks effortless and in reality it feels wonderful.

In trading, those conditions before the trade are called the setup and there are outstanding teachers[19] who can help you learn setups for almost any kind of trading that you want to do. Day Trades. Swing Trades. Time decay trades. They are all fun and can all be profitable.

The more different setups you know the more tools you'll have at your disposal.

But the key thing to remember is that a setup is done ahead of the trade. If you start having that subtle feeling that the trade is slipping away from you, it's time to immediately cut your losses and focus your attention on setting up for the next one.

You can't catch a wave you've missed, so stop paddling and start looking for the next one.

Get Back Up!

You can't catch a wave that's not there,
so don't try.

Anticipation.

It just may be a trader's easiest mistake.

Survival through evolution over the last 200,000 years has bred us as humans to be really good at pattern recognition and be ready to instinctively act when we see something coming that can either be really good or really bad for us.

Unfortunately according to recent research in the emerging science of "neuroeconomics," the same pleasure center in our brains that is affected during sex or drug use is also stimulated in anticipation of "a big payout" so not only do we want to see patterns we really like it when we do.

So it should hardly be surprising that when we begin to watch the cascade of data that is the stock market, we are fooled into anticipating patterns where there are none and trigger our investment decisions on erroneous expectations.

In surfing, you can tell pretty quickly when a wave isn't going to form right or isn't even going to form under you at all.

In trading on the other hand it's a lot harder to know when a good trade is forming up under you. But every successful trader learns how to do this in a way that works for their individual trading style. I've never met a successful trader that uses their feelings or intuition to enter a trade. I've seen lots of people make trades on a hunch or a feeling. But never a long term successful trader. Not a single one.

On the other hand talk to successful traders and they'll be candid that feelings have hurt them more times than they have helped them. What does work for them is gaining objectivity of feedback.

The most successful traders all have a system of objective analysis that has been built ahead of time to tell them when to enter a trade, when to stop out for a minimal loss and when to close a trade in a way that makes them a reasonable profit. When they are trading calmly and like a machine they are at their best. And yes, anyone who tells you that they don't do a little happy dance after a great day is just lying. It feels great but it isn't done by feelings.

If there is any education that you choose to buy, this will most likely be the most important choice you can make. There are some really good teachers[20] out there who have built systems that are terrific for the average investor. With a little practice and applied discipline it can become second nature.

So the next time you feel yourself feel like jumping into a trade because you got a hot tip, or you just know those trends are going to reverse and you want to be ahead of everyone else, just step back from your keyboard, take a breath and remind yourself . . .
. . . you can't catch a wave that's not there, so don't try.

There are many ways to ride.

Long Boards. Short Boards. Boogie Boards. Body Surfing. They all work and they are all fun.

In the same way, I think a good investor works at having a lot of tools at his or her disposal.

Why?

Two reasons. The first is that in a market that is gyrating as wildly as the one we are in, there are times that any one instrument just may not make sense. For example, stocks are great but with the addition of options the risk can be hedged and the rewards can be magnified.

The second reason is, in my experience every new instrument that I learn makes me better at trading the ones I already know about.

I never thought I'd ever want or need to pay attention to the Futures market. That is until someone showed me how the futures can be a wonderful "bird dog" signal for short term trend changes in the equities markets.

I've always said I would pay a lot for the subscription that delivers tomorrow's newspaper today. If someone told you that the Yen Euro cross was an early directional signal for what you were trading would you start learning about currencies?

You bet.

But I can hear you thinking, "Wow, that's a level of investing that is so far beyond me." Well yes and no.

None of these markets are that hard. The people trading them today are no smarter than you. The only difference is that they have just dug in and learned about them. And if you take the long term view and decide that you will add one new instrument or one new strategy to your toolbox every quarter in just a handful of years you'll have a robust tool kit.

That's not to say you will ever even trade commodities for example. But understanding them even at a cursory level can unlock insights that can make you more successful.

Start with whatever interests you and see what feels comfortable. If a paper money[21] account works for you, great. You can try your hand at currencies or futures or commodities without the pain of real losses until you get good enough to try it with your own money.

There are many ways to ride the same wave.

When the Hundred Year Waves show up,
head to the beach.

A lot of the things I've had to say so far are about cutting losses and hedging risk and taking plenty of opportunities to be in cash to miss the big losses. But on the other hand this market is likely a once in a century opportunity.

Yes I said opportunity.

I was living in San Diego when a massive storm blew in what were described as "hundred year waves." It was interesting to see who disappeared from work on "sick leave."

For everyone else that was a dangerous time to be at the beach but for those who recognized it and were ready, this was perhaps an opportunity of a lifetime.

It probably wasn't your best day to rent a board for your first ride, but if you were ready, wow!

This market is the same way. You hear it in the commentary of the talking heads, "The market moved today as far as it would have taken a month to move in the past."

That's not the time to head inland.

It's probably also not the time to be 100% invested unless you really know what you are doing and have ice water in your veins.

But it is the time to take a small chunk of your speculative money and try your hand at riding the big ones.

What's required to win is preparation. One of my mentors has a colorful expression, "The time to prepare for war is in the time of peace." And it's so true. If you're in a time of hundred year waves and your pulse starts racing but you haven't prepared for it, invest no money. You weren't ready and all you'll do is eat sand off the bottom.

But start building strategies and imagining how you would recognize ahead of time that the big ones would be coming. Think through some strategies that you might try. Then look back your charts to those "waterfall" periods and using your back tester[22] to see how those strategies would have done.

Your eyes will pop out on some of them and you'll feel what real greed feels like (yeah I know, that's a new feeling for you. Uh huh.)

But write out your plan and start getting ready.

This is a perfect opportunity for back testing. If you want to back test some different methods there are lots of tools out there. Your broker probably even has one for free so try it.

Pick a time frame where some really huge volatility hit the market and see how you do. Keep practicing until you have a worked out plan for what signals would trigger you to act and your risk management strategy for what you'll do if things don't work out the way you planned.

Then the next time it happens (and it will) take one percent of your portfolio and give it a try.

Then take that learning and prepare a plan for the next big one. Maybe two percent of your portfolio that time.

Pretty soon it will be one of those strategies that you are comfortable with then . . .

. . . when the storms roll in and the hundred year waves show up you'll head to the beach.

Get Back Up!

You can't get anywhere trying to ride
against the wave.

This may be the biggest insight and single best change I have made.

When you surf you paddle out and ride in. To try and ride in the opposite direction of the waves just doesn't work. That's easy to see on the ocean but less clear in the market.

In March of 2008 I was in Las Vegas for an investor conference. At that point, like many others, I was thrashing in the market, making some small gains only to give them up to bigger losses. It was frustrating. And what was even more frustrating was that I could tell that the conference wasn't giving us anything that would make it any better. They were as lost as we were. The only difference was they were still optimistic that "the market would right itself again."

The second evening a bunch of us who were attending went out to dinner together. We all had our game faces on. You know that kind of dinner.

With the exception of one guy.

As we went around the table introducing ourselves and the kind of trading that we were doing he introduced himself as being strongly bearish on the market and that everything in his portfolio was targeted short the market.

I almost levitated across the table to him.

"How can you be that sure?" I asked him.

"I've been studying Elliott Waves for twenty years and it's clear to me that the market will be going well down from here both in the short term but also over the next several years. I'm at this conference to learn how to trade this falling market better." he said.

The room started spinning and it wasn't the wine.

That was what I was missing. It was like Indiana Jones in Raiders of the Lost Ark who turns to his friend Sallah when they realize the measurement that their rival archaeologists are using are wrong and exclaim together, "They're digging in the wrong place!"

It was that kind of Aha! moment.

Now talking about Elliott Wave is often times a controversial subject. People who believe in the essential randomness of the universe (and of markets) often reject Elliott out of hand. People who believe that there is a pattern that threads through the universe often take Elliott as a kind of oracle that can predict the future.

So let me provide some context to my comments. Please hear me out.

First, what was most important for me was not the system and whether it was truly predictive or not but rather that it gave me a whack upside the head and got me considering the market in a different way.

That change of thinking has allowed me to start trading profitably again because my expectations got aligned with the market. The market as it really was, not how I wanted it to be.

Second, by definition there can't be any magical system[2*] that is always right because the market requires two sides to a trade. Someone makes money. Someone loses. As soon as any system gets recognized as being highly predictive a lot of folks crowd in and it can't bear the strain and it stops working.

Sorry.

I wish there was a silver bullet too. But there isn't.

The key learning here is the recognition of when your mindset is working for you and when it isn't. There is a lot of cognitive research[23] that identifies that after we make a decision, our belief in the correctness of that decision gets stronger simply because we made it. After all we are pretty smart aren't we? Over time that reinforcement of self affirmation calcifies and if something changes we are far less likely to see that change because our mind still believes in the condition before the change.

2   I'm using Elliott Wave as a key tool in my toolbox. However I use it as a probabilistic tool rather than a predicative one and that makes all the difference. For more see the end notes.

Notice how the titans of Wall Street, including the demigod of investing Warren Buffet have all taken a shellacking by this market. The surer you are that you are right, the harder it is to see when you are wrong. And the longer that you don't see that, the more you can lose trying.

That doesn't mean to second guess every trade to the point where you are immobilized. But it does mean that it is essential to force yourself to acknowledge what your bias is about the market. Bullish? Bearish? Stagnant? If you don't have a bias you haven't done your homework and have no business trading because you're flying without a flight plan.

But when you do have a bias, at that point you need to be able to answer yourself objectively, whether that bias is giving you better vision for your trades or is it only making you see what you want to see and misdirecting you.

From that objective opinion you can build predetermined strategies for how you will make money in each way the market can go – up, down or sideways.

But above all stay heads up because . . .

. . . you can't get anywhere trying to ride against the wave.

There's no arguing with the Ocean.

Loving what is[24].

It's one of my wife's favorite books and it's also what we have to do in trading.

In surfing that means showing up when the ocean tells us to, not when we decide we want to. It also means surfing the waves that are there not the waves we want to be there.

In trading it's the same way.

You know the feeling when you initiate a trade because it seemed like that was what was called for but the market/ocean seems to change its mind and moves the other way. How do you respond? Do you stick in there, gritting your teeth and try to make it change with your force of will? Do you become frozen, the deer in the headlights watching the trade go farther and farther against you?

Prior to any of those points we need to have decided not to argue,

. . . because there is no arguing with the ocean.

Do we cover, hedge or take off the trade[25]? Do we roll it out in time and hold on? Any of those might be possible.[26]

What is most important is to know ahead of time that a large proportion of our trades are going to just go against us. Sometimes it's because we misread the setup. Other times it was because we traded what we wanted to happen and made ourselves believe. But most of the time things go wrong because they just go wrong.

What matters is whether we are prepared for things going wrong by anticipating in advance how we're going to respond and then having the emotional flexibility to naturally and easily make that responsive action.

One of the trading coaches I regularly listen to[27] has a method for this. He says to give yourself an emotional reward every time a trade goes wrong and you respond by doing the right thing. He laughingly points out that most people would think you were crazy if you tell them that you are rewarding yourself for taking a loss. But great traders know it's true, a quick small loss is your best loss because the winners that you let ride will more than take care of them.

So when you feel like you are wrestling against the universe, stop and remind yourself . . .

. . . there's no arguing with the ocean.

Get Back Up!

It can be painful when you try to shoot the pier. So Don't!

As traders we have to admit it. We like the adrenaline rush of risk.

So I bring up the idea of shooting the pier for us to think about before we are out in the market in a place that's equivalent to being on Huntington Beach and are tempted to shoot the pier.

My reason for bringing this up is that cognitive research points out that we make decisions very differently when we are in a state of arousal[28] than when we aren't. In fact it's actually statistically predictable how far we will overshoot in risky behavior when we are worked up than we would in a rational state of mind. And that difference is a lot.

What that means for me is forewarned is forearmed. We need to build a plan that we will actually follow so we don't make what will be overly risky (meaning dumb) decisions when our decision making ability is impaired and we're in a mental state that is likely to ignore the warnings.

What that plan looks like is different for each individual.

I feel like I'm pretty risk tolerant. My very conservative financial advisor would agree with that. But whew, some of my trading buddies do things that make my head spin. Vive la difference!

What matters to us as traders who want to be successful though are two things. First we need to know ahead of time what level of risk of loss we will be comfortable with after all is said and done. And the measurement for that risk needs to be something that we will agree to no matter whether we are calm or worked up.

Then second, we need to build a conscious plan that we will pay attention to when we are in the heat of the moment.

Most likely the first will change from time to time so revisiting it daily in your trading journal[29] and keeping it front and center in your planning is essential.

The second frankly is a lot harder to do and is also accomplished in that part of your trading journal where you review and critique every trade you make. Why did you make that trade? Honestly. And how did it work out? Again, honestly.

Don't get me wrong. Without risk there can be no reward. But use the pain from risks gone bad to help calibrate the best risk profile for your trading plan. And remember . . .

. . .it can be painful when you try to shoot the pier. So don't!

Get Back Up!

Live to surf. Or surf to live?

You don't have to be a full time trader to be successful. But you will diddle away a LOT of money if you don't treat it like a full time job.

Sorry.

I had an investment teacher a long ways back make the statement, "Treat this like a job and it will reward you like a job. Treat this like an avocation and it will pay you like an avocation." At that point in time that was true, you could make a little money trading a little bit on the side. But it isn't that way any longer. A bear market is crueler than that.

That doesn't mean however that you have to be glued to your trading screen all day. Many of us are still working full time jobs because we're not ready to trade full time.

I met a really great options trader who is still a full time brain surgeon in New York City. No kidding. Sounds like the opening line to a joke but it's true. Most days while the market is open he is in surgery with no way of knowing what's going on in the market. And he is not a simple trader, he's trading complex multi wing[30] spreads.

How does he do it? He is amazingly adept at placing conditional closing orders[31] to take himself out of his trades no matter if they go for him or go against him. He places those conditional orders to close his trades right up front as he is putting the trades on. And he reviews where they are and whether anything has triggered at night after the markets have closed to determine whether he needs to make any changes.

It's a thing of beauty.

That kind of system may be perfect for you. Or it may be totally wrong for you. Neither of those matter.

What does matter is that he has built a trading plan that works full time for him even when he can't pay full time attention to the market. And you can too.

I was so fascinated with what he was doing I had to ask him all about it. As so many great traders are, he was very self effacing and very willing to share. But when I asked him whether he wanted at some point to trade full time he thought for a moment and said, "I don't know really. I love being a surgeon and I can't ever see giving that up. I suppose I may have to some day, but I'm not thinking about that now"

So surf to live or live to surf? It doesn't matter, as long as you have a plan that is working for you full time.

Get Back Up!

Surf from the beach
        before you get on the board.

It's fun to watch what surfers do when they first get to the beach.

They look.

Not at who's there. Or the weather. But at the waves and how they are setting up.

Sometimes after looking out at the horizon for a few minutes they kind of lazily start getting out their gear and chatting up their buds. But other times it's like an alarm bell has just gone off at the firehouse. It's grab the board and beat feet to the water.

Why's that? It's because the experienced surfer knows that there are intangible windows when the weather and tides and whatever kind of karma is out there all come together and the waves are just at their best.

That's when you need to be out on the water sitting on your board and choosing your ride. To be anywhere else is to be missing the party.

Other times it's a matter of choosing among all the pretty good options that are out there.

It's the same with traders.

Call a trader or open up a trader's chat room on any given day with your screens open and you can tell what kind of day it is.

Some days it just feels like everyone's up at the parking lot overlooking the beach or down on the sand shooting the breeze.

Other times you can tell. The serious traders are in the water and getting rides.

The best times to learn are when things change and that alarm bell seems to ring. Look at everything. Where's volume for the day? How about the Advance Decline? TICKS? TRIN? Moving averages rolling over or rolling up?[32]

Don't worry if this all seems like gobbledy gook to you. Just know that these and others are the early warning signs that tell the experienced trader to get in the water and start paddling.

Learn to surf from the beach before you get on your board and you'll learn how to get the better rides.

If a trade starts feeling crowded
it's time to leave. Now!

There's a whole cluster of trading metaphors that center on the fact that smart money knows how to leave a trade by bringing in the, shall we say, less than smart money to hold the bag when a trade is over and ready to decline.

One thing I do know is I am not the smart money. And I've had my share of "holding the bag" as the upside comes to an end.

One thing I have noticed is that there is a definite feeling of crowdedness and almost a party like atmosphere when a trade is about to move down.

I remember hearing a comment by a Wall Street big gun a couple of years back before the real estate market collapsed. He commented that his caddy at a club out on Long Island had asked him for some advice about a spec home he had bought as an investment in California. This big gun asked his caddy if he had ever seen the house he had invested in. The caddy said no but he had been told it was a sure thing. The big gun's comment was, "Right at that moment I knew real estate was about to collapse."

The problem is it's not usually that clear.

Oil in 2008 at $140 per barrel looked sure to go to $200 and anyone that had bet against it before that had gotten killed. But if your last trade was to buy the OIH at $139 you found out how fast the roller coaster rolls over and goes down.

What I've started to do that seems to work is to think about any trade or any investment as being a big room. Look around. If the room feels like it has smart people in it but there are plenty of people outside still questioning whether it's a good idea I'm okay to stay in. But when it starts looking like a party that's too good to be true, that's a warning sign that it probably is and the time to leave was yesterday.

That doesn't mean you can't ride something that is popular and going higher. Just be sure to get more and more nervous and start edging your way towards the door when everyone else is getting more comfortable.

Then when the trade starts feeling crowded it's time to leave. Now!

Get Back Up!

Find the rhythm of the waves you are in.

Like the Roy Orbison lyric you know "when the feelin' an't right."

Timing and balance is everything in surfing from the paddle out, to the selection of the wave, to when and how to pop up, how and when to turn and finally how to end a ride.

It all has to work in harmony with the wave.

The same is true with trading. If I'm trading too tight on a day that's moving in larger swings I get cut off before my trades really get to develop. But if I'm too slow to cut off a loser that just keeps going it can ruin a whole day. Or more.

On the other hand learning how to let winners run until they are through is the key to generating truly large returns over time.

But how do you do that?

I'm convinced that just learning to time entries is

an art unto itself that deserves its own shrine. If it could be reduced to a consistent signal of so many upticks of the TRIN or a certain EMA crossover we'd all be rich by now. But it's not. Like the old adage "you never step into the same river twice" the market is never the same so trading it can't be automated.

Same with exits. It involves a whole bunch of signals but what determines your success is how well you can tell when it's time to leave.

I suppose if I have to be wrong, I'd like to err on the side of keeping smaller gains and enduring smaller losses than the other way around.

But over time you'll learn to . . .

. . .feel the rhythm of the waves you are in.

Lessons from surfing to rebuild your crashed porfolio

Get Back Up!

Practice. Practice. Practice.

One of my mentors has a story about what it takes to learn to be a trader.

It goes something like this when he tells it. "If you need open heart surgery and your cousin Bobby comes up to you and says, 'I just took a weekend course on open heart surgery, how about I do that operation for you?' What would you say? You'd say, 'NO WAY!' Well it's the same with trading. Why does anyone think they can just open a trading account and take a weekend seminar and start making money off of traders who have been doing this for twenty years and are there to eat your lunch? NO WAY!"

That's why he's one of my mentors[33]. After spending twenty years in the CBOE options pits, I'm pretty sure he has a lot to teach me. He's a lifetime learner, always looking for that new and better way and so am I.

But how long will it take before I can expect to get really good at this trading thing? In his intriguing book Outliers[34], Malcom Gladwell is pretty sure he knows and his answer is that it takes ten thousand hours of practice to make the difference between being a talented amateur and being a professional. That's ten years working pretty much full time.

While that may seem intimidating, it actually makes me a lot more comfortable. On the one hand I now have a roadmap – ten thousand hours from when I first made a serious commitment to doing this trading thing, I can reasonably expect to make it my livelihood. I can live with that. If fact I'm really excited to do that because I love it.

On the other hand it helps me to relax and not beat myself up if I'm not mastering this craft in the first year, or the third, or even the fifth year of trading.

I can consistently make money sooner than that and so can you.

But to be a master, yes grasshopper, that will take training from the best that are out there and then a lot of repetition at doing what works again and again until it is your natural habit.

I don't want to get too "wax on wax off" on you, but having a daily, weekly, monthly and annual sequence for your practice is a consistent pattern that I've noticed among long term successful traders.

Like professional athletes they have developed a system of practice and tracking their progress that works for them. An Annual Trading Plan Review is a great place to start. How you set that up is your choice, but if you're stumped there are a number of great traders who offer good starting points.[35]

Likewise, I can tell when I'm staying disciplined by whether I'm keeping my weekly and monthly appointments with myself to track and evaluate my trading progress. Even if I'm getting spanked by the market, when I keep my weekly review and work on revising my plan I know I'm moving forward.

When I delay or gloss over my weekly review I know I'm slacking and only hurting myself and my progress. For me the key to getting back on track is to remember to separate my outcomes from my competency.

The lower my competency the more variable my outcomes. But as my competency improves my outcomes get less and less variable.

And the key to competency is, practice, practice, practice.

Get Back Up!

Sufin' Safari

Let's go surfin' now
Everybody's learning how
Come on and safari with me.
<small>LYRICS BY BRAIN WILSON AND MIKE LOVE</small>

Learning to be a great trader is a self managed curriculum. So who to learn from?

The first piece of good news is that there are a ton of folks who want to educate you. Some are good. Others have just been lucky and only think they know what they're talking about. Others are just big talkers. But the good ones are worth their weight in gold and worth the search to find them.

The second piece of good news is that there is no Ivy League of trading schools that is the exclusive source of secret knowledge that only the elite can enter. Quite the opposite. There are great courses and trainers and mentors out there, with even more new ones showing up every day challenging the establishment with new and better ways of teaching.

I think there are three easy screening criteria to help you decide who to learn from.

The first is philosophical. You should learn something from everyone but you shouldn't pay everyone to learn. There will be a lot of times you will learn what not to do by watching others fall on their nose with that system. But even that is learning that can help you not waste your time with those mistakes. It is important however that you NOT pay anyone for that. Learn something from everyone you come across. But save your education funds for what will teach you how to make money in a way that works for you.

The second criterion is to only pay for learning when you are confident that the method is transferable. Are there a significant number of people like you who have learned to be successful over several years from that course or mentor? Can they tell you how they are doing it in a way that you can understand and see yourself actually doing? Are they personally still being successful today in this bear market? If not, it's probably not for you so keep looking.

Third and most important. Will they teach you the basics of their approach well enough for free that you can really tell what you will be getting from your education? If the secret sauce is behind a curtain that you can't get to until they have your money walk away. No questions no quibbling, just walk away.

The reason for that, is there is nothing really new to the craft of trading. I mean it. Really.

There may be some approaches that are a little

more refined, or some specialized tools that make an approach a little more automated but the basics of trading have been with us as long as there have been markets. This is a craft that must be learned and the money is made by working the craft not some exotic secret indicator that will tell you when to buy and when to sell.

Sorry. Anyone who tries to tell you otherwise is just selling you snake oil.

But those three screening criteria actually open up a wealth of learning opportunities. Anyone who makes money each time you trade will have a ton of education available for you for free. Many of the exchanges[36] have educational portals as do all of the online brokers. Most successful traders I know have a number of accounts open across a number of brokers because they have learned their way through the educational materials provided. It's up to each broker to keep improving their tools and training to keep earning your commissions and the good ones do.

So start laying out your education plan to meet your trading plan and get started on your . . .

     . . . surfing safari.

Get Back Up!

It's a solitary sport . . .
but you do it better with friends around.

Trading as a profession is like being a hunter gatherer in the wilderness.

The traits and skills that you may have learned to be successful in a modern profession, particularly those in modern corporations are unsuitable and probably detrimental to your success as a trader.

What's confusing for a lot of people is that their experience of investing is largely from managing their retirement accounts, working with a professional advisor who manages their holdings for them. Most people's experience is working with an advisor who guides them to decisions that are then delegated to an organization where professionals who they never actually see, do things for them that they really don't understand.

However when you are a self managed investor it's just you and your trading account against the world.

If a trade is going to be made, you have to decide what to do and when to do it. Just you and your trading screen.

No wonder there are so many people who swarm to follow trading gurus and buy advisory services to guide their trading. As people raised in modern interdependent societies we are used to operating as members of an organization. Organizations move together and operate by consensus. Hunter gathers operate alone and eat what they kill.

Being out in the cold on your own is scary.

But it's what is.

However once we realize that and stop looking for the guru to follow, we open ourselves up to something else. Finding others to hunt along side with can be an amazing resource.

Finding other traders to share with and learn from is good but my experience, and it's shared by some of the best teachers I know, is that finding a shared accountability group is by far the best.

What are they like? One group I know from Atlanta meets every trading day at one member's house. They all have their trading screens open and they discuss setups, entries and exits. Sometimes they do the same trades sometimes they all do different trades. No one is in charge and no one leads. They just benefit by watching and learning from each other.

My trading group meets virtually, online every Tuesday night. That's because we are spread from Manhattan to Vancouver, B.C. to Guatemala. We teleconference and use desktop sharing software to conduct our meetings and show each other our trades. Both the ones that aren't working as well as the ones that are.

We stay in touch daily via a private Yahoo mail group where everyone comments and shares market insights and asks questions. Again, we have no leader. We have decided consciously to operate by the principles of Open Space[37] where decisions are shared and anyone can "vote with their feet."

But we are also mutually accountable. We notice when someone seems to have dropped out and we call them up and offer encouragement and support.

Likewise during times of breaking news the emails and phone calls fly so no one gets left out on a major market move. And on days when the market is out to smash you it's good to have lots of eyes looking out for the group's best interest.

How do you find a trading group? Our group found each other by going out to dinner together during a trading seminar that we were all attending. The two keys for us were that we had been in the same course together so we had a common set of understanding and approach to trading. Over that first dinner in San Diego we got honest with each other about what was and wasn't working for us and that candor has carried through in our relationships to this day.

That openness and realization that we could help ourselves by helping each other got us going.

There are lots of ways to find a group, the key is to find one.

It's a solitary sport . . . but you do it better with friends around.

Get Back Up!

It's more than a ride. It's a lifestyle.

You know the old adage about teaching a man to fish and he'll never be hungry. This book takes that approach. It's about how to think rather than a set of cookbook recipes that may work for some people but not be right for you.

What I've noticed is that no single approach or set of strategies is right for everyone. And the strategies that are working for us today probably will stop working at some point and the quicker we realize that and shift to something else the better our portfolios will thrive over the long run.

And in reality that's what I'm looking for.

For every surfer there have been rides that felt so perfect there just couldn't be anything finer. And for that matter there have been trades that you just want to relive again and again.

What I'm looking for is a lifestyle that naturally and easily heads down to the beach (the market) every day.

From the parking I and my buddies scout out the sets and decide whether to ride there or head down the coast to where we hear the patterns are better.

If it's not a great day to ride/trade I'm content because my life is more than one ride. My life is more than one day or even one perfect summer. It's a fulfilling and comfortable lifestyle that enjoys different conditions and different seasons but loves to ride them all, regardless of how and when they come to me.

If that's what you're looking for in trading and in life then great, let's share some thoughts. I've shared mine here and I hope you share yours with me online at www.fromsurfing.com.

Thanks for stepping into this journey. My hope for you is that when you're done it's more than a ride, it's a lifestyle.

Notes and References

1 **How can we know this is long term Bear Market?** The difference this time is that this Bear was triggered by the biggest credit bubble in 100 years. So the duration and depths of this Bear will be huge. For current perspectives on Where in the Bear Are We? see the companion website www.fromsurfing.com .

2 A **position** is the amount of a security such as stock or an that has been bought (which constitutes a long position) or sold short (which constitutes a short position). In other words, it's a trade an investor currently has open. For more on "short" see page 18.

3 **Where in the Bear Are We?**
It is virtually undisputed that we are in a Bear Market. However at any point in time there are three crucial questions that are extremely unclear. How long will the down trend continue? How far down will it go? And most importantly over the period we expect to be in a trade (minutes, days or weeks), will the market move with the

trend (down) or in a counter trend move (up)?

For a time frame of day or weeks using an Elliott Wave perspective as a starting point is useful place to start.

There are a number of Elliott Wave based analysts out there but the leading authority seems to be Elliott Wave International. You can find their website at www. elliottwave. com/.

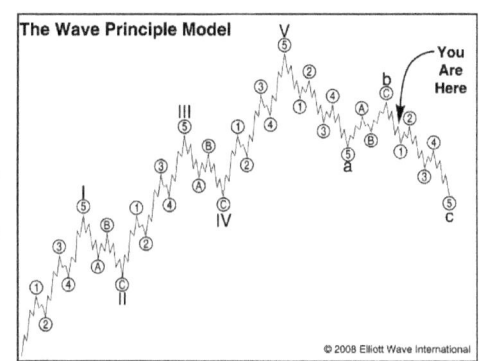

Ralph Nelson Elliott developed this trend analysis approach in the 1930's by recognizing that social, or crowd, behavior trends and reverses in recognizable patterns. Using stock market data as his main research tool, Elliott isolated thirteen patterns of movement, or "waves," that recur in market price data. He named, defined and illustrated those patterns then described how these patterns link together into larger patterns.

It would be nice to know the future. But we can't. While the Wave Principle cannot provide certainty about any one market outcome; what it can do is provide an objective means of assessing the relative probabilities of possible future paths for the market.

From there, your own market judgment has to take over. Why do you agree or disagree with the current projection and how will your trade it? If you're wrong what will you use to decide and what will you do then?

Key books are:

Elliott Wave Principle: Key to Market Behavior by A.J. Frost & Robert R. Prechter, Jr. Published by John Wiley & Sons, 10th Edition, 2001.

Conquer the Crash: You Can Survive and Prosper in a Deflationary Depression by Robert R. Prechter, Jr, John Wiley and Sons, 2002

4 When you really understand what got us into this bear market you'll be better at recognizing when it can be over.

No matter how bad you think the credit crisis is, it's probably worse than you can conceive of. I'm not kidding.

Unlike the pundits who have identified the culprits who created the financial instruments that have plundered world economies after the fact, Charles Morris was curmudgeonly enough to have written this book before it actually unfolded. At the time this was published he was generally regarded as an alarmist.

Morris identifies the eight steps to a multi trillion dollar meltdown:
1. The Fed spikes the punch bowl
2. Leverage soars
3. Consumers throw a toga party
4. A dollar tsunami
5. Yields plummet
6. Hedge funds peddle crystal meth
7. A ratings antigravity machine
8. The Wile E. Coyote moment arrives

Morris's only shortcoming in his assesment was that even he underestimated how bad it could get. *The Two Trillion Dollar Meltdown: Easy Money, High Rollers, and the Great Credit Crash* by Charles R. Morris, PublicAffairs; Revised edition 2009.

5   **A retail investor** is anyone who buys and sells securities on their own behalf--not for an organization.

6   In case you are unsure about what these securities are here's a quick description of each. For more detailed information a good source is www.investopedia.com. Stock means a share of ownership in a corporation. As an owner you have the right to vote on issues presented at the company meeting in proportion to the shares you own and receive dividends if you own shares on the date they are paid.

An **option** is a contract written by a seller that conveys to the buyer the right — but not the obligation — to buy (in the case of a call option) or to sell (in the case of a put option) a particular asset, such as shares of stock or some other underlying security, within a certain time period. In return for granting the option, the seller collects a payment (the premium) from the buyer.

Currencies are just what you'd expect, the form of money from different countries around the world. The foreign exchange (currency, ForEx, or FX) market is where currency trading takes place. The forex market is the largest, most liquid market in the world with an average traded value that exceeds $1.9 trillion per day and includes all of the currencies in the world. FX transactions typically involve one party purchasing a quantity of one currency in exchange for paying a quantity of another.

Commodity markets are markets where raw or primary products are exchanged. These raw commodities are traded on regulated commodities exchanges, in which they are bought and sold in standardized contracts.

7 **Market makers** are the people you see in the exchange pits who are facilitating transactions between buyers and sellers. They specialize in a single security, currency or commodity and transact million of dollars in a typical day. Their role is to keep markets moving (liquid) and to take a tiny spread (profit) on the difference between what they buy and sell.

8 **The Chicago Board Of Options Exchange (CBOE)** is the largest U.S. options exchange. Options are traded on over 2,200 companies, 22 stock indexes, and 140 exchange-traded funds (ETFs).

9 By **cash** I mean the monetary value in an investment account that is not invested in a security. As such it can neither gain or lose value. Cash (dollars or euros or yen depending on the country where the account is held) in an investment account will most likely be held in money market funds and can be available at any time to invest or trade. Going to cash means selling a security but keeping the monetary value in the investment account.

10 **Volatility** refers to the statistical potential for unpredictable change over time. It is at the heart of modeling risk. In high volatility periods there is high risk but high possible reward. In low volatility periods the risk is lower but the potential for rewards are lower as well.

11 Every investor or trader uses different **market signals** to help them decide when is a good time to buy or sell. There may literally be thousands of different indicators

out there but they all boil down to two things. The price history and the quantity history of the security is being tracked. Virtually all indicators then make calculations based on the rate of change and the difference in the rate of change of price and volume over time. Some examples are simple moving averages (SMA)

12   Dennis Gartman

This quote on page 21 is by memory from Dennis Gartman. Anyone who trades anything will recognize the experience and insight of Dennis Gartman commentary. This particular quote was from one of his many appearances on fast Money on CNBC. For those who can afford it, The Gartman Letter is a daily commentary on the global capital markets subscribed to by leading banks, broking firms, hedge funds, mutual funds, energy and grain trading companies around the world. http://www. thegartmanletter.com

For the rest of us, be on the lookout for his many appearances both on air and at investing conferences and then every week or so do a Google News search and you'll pick up another handful of great insights.

13   Swing traders try to capture gains in a security within one to four days. Large institutions trade in sizes too big to move in and out of stocks quickly so an individual trader is often able to exploit short-term stock movements without the competition of major traders.

Day Traders try to capture gains in a security within a single trading day. This can occur in any marketplace but is most common in the foreign-exchange (forex) market and stock market. Typically, day traders utilize high amounts of leverage and short-term trading strategies to capitalize on small price movements in highly liquid stocks or currencies making many trades in a day but closing all trades before the close of the market.

14 An **options spread** is a trade that uses two options that are different in kind (puts and calls) or price or time periods to either hedge risk or to make money from the difference in how the options gain or lose value over time in combination with each other.

15 **Fundamental analysis** examines dividends paid, operating cash flow, capital financing, earnings estimates and growth rate projections to help a trader decide what a stock price should be. An fundamentals driven investor believes that markets may misprice a security in the short run but that the "correct" price will eventually be reached.

16 **Technical analysis** considers only the actual price and volume behavior of the market or instrument. Traders driven by technical analysis use models and trading rules based on price and volume change, such as moving averages, regressions, and recognition of chart patterns.

17 The **spread** of a stock price is the difference between the bid (price to buy) and the ask (the price to sell) a security such as a stock or an option. The spread is the profit that a market maker (see end note 7) takes on a transaction. Securities that have low volume can charge wider spreads say ten to 30 cents per share. But securities that are very large and are very liquid often have spreads between the buy and sell price of as little as a cent and are referred to as penny wide spreads. Obviously the tighter the spread the less is lost to transaction costs.

18   **Market sectors** are groupings of businesses that are buying and selling goods and services that they are in direct competition with each other. Analysts divide the stock market itself into market sectors so that the prices and market performance of companies that are in direct competition can be looked at as a whole and the individual companies can be compared.

Sector rotation is a strategy sometimes used by large institutional investors who believe that as the broader market goes through growth and recession cycles that certain sectors will do better in different economic conditions. Commentators will observe that money seems to be rotation into a sector, say semiconductors or out of a sector say primary metals.

19   **Setups**
Outside of dumb luck the basis for success of any trade can usually be attributed to the quality of the setup. Is the trade well conceived ahead of time, consistently applied and honestly evaluated after the trade is closed? If so you can usually make a profit.

While there are literally hundreds of great trading teachers out there, two sources that are very useful in learning setups are:

Shadow Trader

Want to listen in and watch day traders in action for free? Better yet, want to get free lessons in the trading tools they use? Chief Equity Strategist, Peter Reznicek of Shadow Trader offers daily trading newsletters and advisories on a subscription basis for both general market equities and currencies. For the free recorded video lessons go to http://www.shadowtrader.net/ and check out the Education button under the Archives tab.

ShadowTrader Squawk Box is a professional live audio and video broadcast offering successful stock and option traders and investors of any level the tools and guidance desired to navigate the market and be more successful trading it. The broadcast provides useful market commentary to its trading audience in real time. To listen in and watch you need to have an active ThinkOrSwim trading account http://www.thinkorswim.com. On any given day there are over a thousand traders listening in to the broadcast and writing in to the chat.

Mastering the Trade
One of the best books on setups and on day trading in general is **Mastering the Trade** by John F. Carter, McGraw-Hill Trader's Edge 2005. Even if you never expect to day trade but are just going to swing trade learning John's setups will make you a much more powerful and successful trader.

20   Another great teacher who has a very straightforward and practical system of trading is Robert Miner. His book High Probability Trading Strategies: Entry to Exit Tactics for the Forex, Futures, and Stock Markets by Robert C. Miner, Wiley Trading, 2008 is excellent and contains an audio visual companion cd. Even better in my estimation is his full audio video trading course Dynamic Trading Multimedia E-Learning Workshop http://www.dynamictraders.com/education/e-learning.html. It's pricey but well worth it.

21 A **paper money** or practice training account is an account at a brokerage firm that operates identically to a regular trading account but all of the transactions are simulated using the equivalent of monopoly money. It's a great way to learn how to trade without losing any of your own money while you are making your beginner's mistakes. You'll likely find that even after you are an experienced trader that you'll return to your paper money account when you want to try something new out and don't want to make mistakes with real money.

I should probably also pass on some of the best advice that my mentor Dan Sheridan ever gave me. And that is, don't try and move from a paper money account to trading a fully funded account with a substantial portion of your money in it. Instead, trade a very small account using only say $5,000 until you have proved to yourself that you can make money in that account as well.

having real money on the line just makes people trade differently and like me (and my wife) you'll thank Dan for having you lose only hundreds instead of thousands on your training wheels.

22   **Back Testing Tools**
The state of online trading tools is constantly changing. At the risk of being out dated here are three back testing tools to check out ranging from free to pricey.

Strategy Desk from TD Ameritrade is an all purpose back testing platform for testing stock strategies in timeframes as small as a second. There are no futures, commodities or options, but it's a free download when you have a TD Ameritrade account. http://www.tdameritrade.com.

ThinkBack from ThinkOrSwim is a free back testing platform built right in to the TOS platform that can back test strategies for stocks, options, futures, currencies and even pairs trades. The two limitations as of this writing are that it can only test for day time frames and it lacks a spiffy charting package so you can't see the price action in a graphical format. www.thinkorswim.com.

OptionVue from Optionvue Systems International is one of the most sophisticated Back Trading platforms available for stocks, options and commodities. With OptionVue you can test multiple strategies at the same time in time frames as small as 15 minutes. It is however subscription based with increasing price levels for different data services. www.otionvue.com

23 **The illusion of feeling stronger** about a decision after we make it is described in *Your Money and Your Brain: How the New Science of Neuroeconomics Can Help Make You Rich* by Jason Zweig, Simon & Schuster, 2007. In his fascinating Zweig identifies how, among other things when it comes to investments, we are mostly too confident in our own abilities which itself leads to overconfidence. For example, we believe that our own selected lottery ticket has a better chance of winning than someone else's selected ticket even though all of us know that the odds are the same for everyone. Your portfolio will thank you for reading this book.

24 *Loving What Is: Four Questions That Can Change Your Life* by Byron Katie and Stephen Mitchell, Three Rivers Press, 2003
While this book has nothing to do with trading, the "'work" that Byron Katie asks you to do in this book is the mental exercise of seeing what really is and dealing with it. The core is a series of four questions addressed to examine unhelpful preconceptions and what you will do about them. While this book may help in your personal

life, when applied to trading the four questions style of perceiving can develop the habitual clarity and objectivity we need to have towards our trades to be successful.

25   **Covering the trade**, is the action of completing a trade particularly when you have placed a short trade (sold an equity that you don't own) and need to buy the equity to close the trade (hopefully at a lower price than what you sold it for). Yes it's possible to sell high and then buy it lower afterwards (also referred to as borrowing).

Hedging the trade is the action of adding additional instruments, for instance put or call options on a stock, to offset a potential decline in price (the options gain value as the stock loses value) and your investment holds its value in spite of the market declining. For more information see http://www.marketamer.com/.

26   **Adjusting the trade**
The methods of adjusting a losing trade into a winning strategy instead of just closing it is taught by **Spread Trade Systems** www.spreadtradesystems.com. This is a fee based online educational community that provides a systematic education in basic options, spreads and risk hedging. Courses are available as on-demand prerecorded classes combined with live, online classes, conducted in a virtual classroom with an instructor who guides the discussion and augmented by live chats and a weekly online radio show for enrolled students and graduates.

27   **Coaches**
Getting good coaching can make the life of a trader less lonely and a lot more successful. One of my favorite ways to get coaching is by podcast because I can get out from behind my trading screen and take a hike with the dogs

while reenergizing my mind. Even though it's primarily targeted to day traders, The Mind of a Trader Podcast by Steve Croft is a weekly session that can help you step back and reexamine what you are doing and how you can be doing better. Available free from iTunes or www.tradingpostfinancial.com/blog/categories/mind-of-a-trader

If you have coaches that you think are great share them with me at www.fromsurfing.com

28   MIT professor Dan Ariely has discovered from 20 years of researching behavioral economics, people tend to behave irrationally in a predictable fashion. But since it's predictable we can recognize our irrational tendencies and break through these systematic patterns of thought to make better decisions. *Predictably Irrational: The Hidden Forces That Shape Our Decisions* by Dan Ariely, HarperCollins, 2008.

29   Keeping a **Daily Trading Journal** that is part of a weekly, monthly and annual trading plan is an essential discipline for staying on track and not losing your way. John Carter has excellent chapters in Mastering The Trade (referenced in note 19 above) on building a plan and working your daily journal. The old saw "Failing to plan is planning to fail" is a hard lesson for swashbuckling traders but a lesson we all learn eventually. I find that my both my plans and the formats for my daily journal continue to morph over time as my approach and competence has matured. The key is write something down now if you aren't doing this and refine it over time. But get started now. Yes I mean right now before you read another thing. You'll be glad you did.

30 A **multi wing spread** is an advanced options strategy that involves buying and holding four different options with different strike prices but the same expiration date. The potential for profit or loss is limited in this strategy by the hedge of the options against each other.

31 A **conditional closing order** sets the conditions for when and how an open trade will be closed such as when a security meets a preset price or limit of loss. After the conditional order is placed it waits to execute when the conditions are met whether you have your account running or not.

32 These are all part of the set of tools that monitor **market internals.** You can think of them like the readouts on the dashboard of your car, or if you fly your instrument console of your plane. The various advance decline ratios track whether rising issues are outpacing declining issues to signal market direction. When the TICKS (the measure of purchases made on the bid or the ask) are gyrating dramatically up or down is another signal of whether there is frenzy in market orders and the direction it's headed, for the moment. Most important are the moving averages and momentum indicators. These are key signals to let you know where the market is trending over the last minute, hour, day, week and month. Get to know and get comfortable with all of them and you'll feel like a pilot with good instruments in a fog rather than wondering if you are flying blind and if there could be a mountain up ahead.

33 Mentoring
I can't stress enough the impact that having a mentor can make on your trading success. Almost all star athletes can point to mentor as being crucial to their career for good reason. No matter how great the talent

a good mentor has the experience to help us see our performance objectively and guide our improvement as we learn the skills to attain mastery.

I mostly trade stock options and am looking at generating monthly income so I chose a 22 year veteran trader from the Chicago Options pits as my mentor, **Dan Sheridan – Sheridan Option Mentoring**

Whoever you choose, make sure that they have a track record of making money in all kinds of markets and that they have a mentor's heart. That's a rare combination. There are a lot of successful traders but they are too caught up in themselves to look out for your best interest. And there are a lot of caring folks who have the lingo down but couldn't trade their way out of a wet paper bag. Dan met those criteria and more for me. The benefit that I wasn't counting on, but has been hugely helpful, is the community of traders in the Sheridan learning community. For more information www. sheridanmentoring.com.

If you have a great mentor share them with us at www. fromsurfing.com. We all can use all the help we can get.

34 *Outliers: The Story of Success* by Malcolm Gladwell, Little, Brown and Company, 2008.

35 *Come Into My Trading Room: A Complete Guide to Trading* by Alexander Elder, Wiley, 2002 is a great guide that includes developing a trading plan and goes all the way through organizing your time.

36 For options the CBOE (Chicago Board of Options Exchange) has a terrific series of classes on a wide variety of topics featuring recognized experts in options trading. www.cboe.com/

37 **Open Space** is a simple means to self-organize any group without the pressure of being or having a "leader." My favorite Open Space principle is The Law of Two Feet: "If you find yourself in a situation where you aren't learning or contributing, go somewhere else." From the law, flow four principles:

> Whoever comes are the right people
> Whatever happens is the only thing that could have
> Whenever it starts is the right time
> When it's over, it's over

Our group finds that it's a great way to manage ourselves and eliminates a lot of the interpersonal static that gets in the way when people try to work together.

Open Space Technology: A User's Guide by Harrison Owen Berrett-Koehler Publishers; 3rd edition, 2008

Get Back Up!

Oh yeah. What was the best advice I ever got
about surfing?

Shut up and ride.